Gentleman Jim
AND THE
Great John L.

Story and Pictures by
SYD HOFF

A Break-of-Day Book
Coward, McCann & Geoghegan, Inc.
New York

FOR MY SISTER DOROTHY

Published simultaneously in Canada by
Longman Canada Limited, Toronto.
ISBN 0-698-30669-4

Library of Congress Cataloging in Publication Data
Hoff, Sydney, 1912-
    Gentleman Jim and the great John L.
    (A Break-of-day book)
    SUMMARY: Briefly recounts the events of the
1892 boxing match between heavyweight champion
John L. Sullivan and challenger "Gentleman Jim"
Corbett.
    1. Sullivan, John Lawrence, 1858-1918—
Juvenile literature. 2. Corbett, James John,
1866-1933—Juvenile literature. 3. Boxers (Sports)
—United States—Biography—Juvenile literature.
[1. Sullivan, John Lawrence, 1858-1918.
2. Corbett, James John, 1866-1933. 3. Boxers
(Sports)] I. Title.
GV1132.S95H63   796.8'3'0922 [B] [920]
                                        77-175

Printed in the United States of America

Color separations by Harriet Sherman

This is the true story of two prizefighters and their historic battle for the heavyweight championship of the world in 1891. John L. Sullivan spent the last years of his life as a stage actor, and a crusader against hard liquor. James J. Corbett, always a believer in clean living, became an actor too, and remained a model for many young fighters who followed him.

Long ago in Boston there lived a
rough, tough fighter
who could hardly read or write.

4

His name was John L. Sullivan,
and pictures of him
hung all over the city.

"I can lick any man in the world,"
said Sullivan as he walked
down the street,
flinging coins to the children.

6

Grown men followed him.
Ladies dropped flowers
at his feet.
They loved him because he was
"the Boston Strong Boy,"
heavyweight champion
of the world.

They saw Sullivan
hoist a policeman
way up high in the air,
over his head.

8

They saw him bend iron horseshoes
with his bare hands.

"Hoo-ray for the Great John L.!"
they shouted when he went in
some place to eat and drink
where music played and
Irish voices filled the air with songs.

10

Strangers pushed close to Sullivan
with hard-luck stories,
hoping to wheedle money out of him,
or just to shake hands with him

so friends could later say
they shook the hand
that shook the hand
of the Great John L.

13

John L. Sullivan fought
over two hundred men
and beat them all.
In those days
fighters did not wear gloves
and they fought to the finish.
In many places
fighting was against the law.
So Sullivan fought
wherever he could—
on river barges, in stables,
on the stages of theaters.

Sometimes a match would be
stopped in the middle.
Everyone would run
from the police
to keep from being arrested.

15

Sometimes a bout
had to be continued
on an open field or farm,
with cows and chickens watching.

But they always ended the same way,
with the Boston Strong Boy
standing over his fallen foe
and the crowd shouting
"Hoor-ray for the Great John L.!"

"All I have to do is look at them
and they fall down,"
boasted Sullivan.

He spent less and less
of his time training,
and more and more
of his time eating and drinking.

He ate and drank so much
that everyone wondered
where he put it all.

When it grew late
and the Boston Strong Boy
could eat and drink no more,
he got into his carriage
and was driven home.

Servants put him to bed
and tucked him under silk covers.
"I can lick any man in the world,"
he mumbled.
"All I have to do is look at them
and they fall down."

One day John L. Sullivan
was eating and drinking as usual,
instead of training.
A newsboy shouted in the street,
"James J. Corbett wins again!
Will meet Sullivan in the ring next!"

Everybody laughed.

But one man
who had seen Corbett
in the ring, said,
"Gentleman Jim
is not just a fighter,
he's a *boxer*.
He won't just stand still
in one spot
and let himself get hit."

"He will bob and weave.
He will dance around the ring
and wear the champ down.
Then he will go
for the knockout himself."

They threw the man
out of the place.

John L. Sullivan ordered
more food and drink for everyone.
People moved closer to him.

"I can lick any man in the world,"
he said.
"Especially a bank clerk
named Corbett
from San Francisco."

Fat and flabby, John L. Sullivan
stepped into the ring
in New Orleans
on September 7, 1892
for the great showdown.
Fighting was legal in that city
and fighters wore gloves.
The crowd was 10,000 strong.

"Hoo-ray for the Great John L.,"
everyone shouted.

They hardly paid any attention
to the challenger.
He weighed in
at only 180 pounds
compared to the champ's 212.

The fight began
and the Great John L.
swung his mighty
sledgehammer right.

Gentleman Jim stepped
nimbly out of reach.

The Great John L.
now swung the left that had brought
two hundred men to their knees.

He missed by a mile.

The Boston Strong Boy
kept swinging and swinging.
Corbett just kept dancing
out of reach
while the crowd booed him.

"Sir, is that the best you can do?"
he asked Sullivan politely.

Soon the Great John L.
was gasping for breath.
He didn't look so great anymore.
"Stand in one place like a man
and let me hit you," he wheezed.

But all James Corbett did was
jab him in the ribs.

In the seventeenth round
Gentleman Jim
was hitting the champion
hard enough to fell an oak tree.
But John L. Sullivan
still stood there,
refusing to fall.

At last the Great John L.
went down in the twenty-first round.
He could rise to his feet no more.

The referee counted to ten
and raised James J. Corbett's arm
in victory.
The world had a new
heavyweight champion.

Ten thousand people were silent
as John L. Sullivan
lifted himself to the ropes.
He said for all to hear,
"If I had to lose,
I'm glad it was to Gentleman Jim."

The Boston Strong Boy
wasn't too sorry that crowds
no longer followed him
down the street.
Or that he couldn't go on saying,
"I can lick any man in the world."

There was still
plenty to eat and drink.
And there were always
enough people around to shout
"Hoo-ray for the Great John L.!"

THE END

38452

JE
HOFF
   GENTLEMAN JIM AND THE GREAT
JOHN L
           4.69

N/U last 4yrs 5-9/10 12 circs 8 libs